Ancient Roman Children

Richard Tames

Heinemann Library
Chicago, Illinois

Customer Service 888-454-2279
Visit our website at www.heinemannlibrary.com

Designed by Tinstar Design
Illustrated by Jeff Edwards
Originated by Ambassador Litho
Printed by Wing King Tong in Hong Kong, China

07 06 05 04 03
10 9 8 7 6 5 4 3 2 1   NOV 0 8 2003

Library of Congress Cataloging-in-Publication Data
Tames, Richard.
  Ancient Roman children / Richard Tames.
    p. cm. -- (People in the past)
Summary: Presents an account of life in ancient Rome from a child's perspective, discussing language, religion, weddings, funeral customs, and more.
Includes bibliographical references and index.
  ISBN 1-58810-634-9 (lib. bbg.) -- ISBN 1-40340-518-2 (pbk.)
  1. Children--Rome--Social conditions--Juvenile literature. 2.Children--Rome--Social life and customs--Juvenile literature. 3. Rome--Civilization--Juvenile literature. [1. Rome--Social life and customs. 2. Rome--Civilization.] I. Title. II. Series.
  HQ792.R83 T35 2002
  305.23'0937--dc21
                                2002005696

Acknowledgments

The author and publishers are grateful to the following for permission to reproduce copyright material: pp. 6, 7, 16, 20, 22, 26, 27, 30, 41 Ancient Art & Architecture Collection; pp. 8, 39 C. M. Dixon; pp. 9, 10, 12, 24 Scala Art Resource; p. 14 Art Directors & TRIP/Carlos Chinca ;p. 15 Colchester Museums; pp. 17, 34 John Seely; pp. 18, 23, 28 AKG Photos; p. 25 English Heritage Photo Library/Corbridge Museum; p. 29 Trevor Clifford; p. 32 Sonia Halliday; pp. 36, 38 Werner Foreman Archive; p. 40 Michael Holford; pp. 42, 43 Museum of London Archaeological Service.

Cover photograph by Corbis.

Every effort has been made to contact copyright holders of any material reproduced in this book. Any omissions will be rectified in subsequent printings if notice is given to the publisher.

Some words are shown in bold, **like this.** You can find out what they mean by looking in the glossary.

Contents

The Roman World

From city to empire

Ancient Rome began as a city and grew into an **empire,** stretching from Italy as far as Scotland, Spain, Sudan, and Syria. As Rome's empire expanded, so did Roman law and Rome's language, Latin.

As the capital of the empire, Rome was the center of its excellent road system. It grew to become a city of a million people, by far the largest in the Roman world. Respect for the **emperor,** obedience to Roman law, and excellently trained Roman armies held the huge empire together. For centuries the enormous army protected the empire against **barbarian** raiders on its borders.

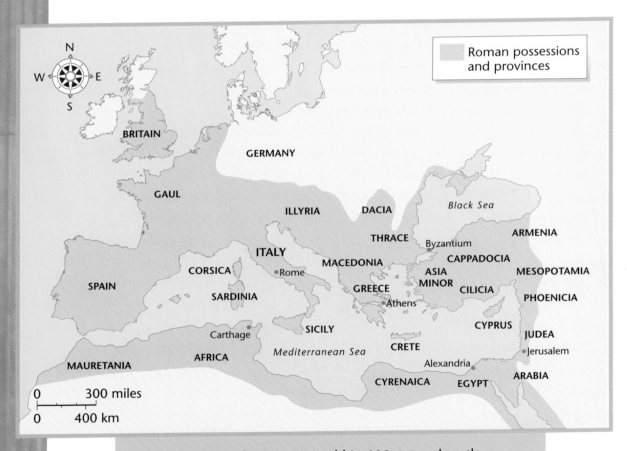

This map shows the Roman world in 100 C.E., when the empire was at its biggest. In many lands, families under Roman rule copied Roman ways, and lived in Roman-style homes.

Latin, languages, and learning

Roman civilization lasted over a thousand years. Latin, the Roman language, later developed into other languages including Italian, French, Spanish, Portuguese, and Rumanian. Even English, a **Germanic** language, owes a third of its words to Latin. Some, like "exit" (he goes), or "veto" (I forbid) are written exactly the way a Roman would have written them. Latin remained the language educated people had to learn throughout Europe until about 1800. It still remains the official language of the Roman Catholic Church to this day. Species of plants, birds, and animals are still recognized around the world by their Latin names.

Rome all around

Modern roads still follow routes first surveyed and built by Roman engineers. In Britain they built 6,000 miles (9,656 kilometers) of roads within 40 years of their conquest. Many sections of Roman city walls still stand. London, Paris, and Milan were all founded by Romans. Most European countries' legal systems are still based on Roman law. Roman history has inspired plays by Shakespeare, operas by Verdi, and films by Hollywood. We can also thank the Romans for banks, crews of fire fighters, and public hospitals. They also gave us apartment buildings and sewer systems, as well as central heating, glass windows, concrete, and our calendar.

Rome's children

The Romans liked to have large families, with many children. Unfortunately, many children did not live to be old enough to marry and have children of their own. We know a lot less about the lives of Roman children than we do about their parents. This book is about explaining why this is, and what we do know.

Invisible Children of Rome

One way to find out about Roman children is by reading what people wrote about them. Some important Roman writers like Horace, Cicero, and Pliny did write about children. However, they wrote from an adult's point of view. Usually they wrote about how children should behave, rather than how they actually did behave. Women spent more time with children than men did, but women rarely wrote. Roman laws set out the rights and duties of children in detail. The laws, however, are more evidence of how life should have been, rather than how it really was.

Time warp

In 79 C.E., a volcanic eruption of Mount Vesuvius destroyed the seaside towns of Pompeii and Herculaneum. Buildings, as well as bodies, were buried beneath a layer of lava over thirteen feet (4 meters) deep. Pliny the Younger, an eyewitness, described the event in two letters to the historian Tacitus. **Excavations** that began in the 1700s have uncovered half of Pompeii, including documents preserved in a chest, and paintings on walls. These finds tell us about the lives of Roman families and children.

The homes of rich Romans were decorated with wall paintings, like this one, often showing scenes from everyday life—but not the everyday life of the poor.

This statue shows Romulus and Remus as babies, with the she-wolf who brought them up.

Recovering the past

Pompeii was a resort town where many wealthy Romans had homes for vacations or their retirement. This means that what has been found there may not be typical of the way of life for the average Roman. Excavations of poor people's homes in the port of Ostia, near Rome, probably provide better evidence of this.

Romulus and Remus

Roman **myths,** like the one about Romulus and Remus, the legendary founders of Rome, also show Roman ideas about childhood. The twin brothers were left to die at birth, but were brought up by a wolf. When they grew up, they built a city where the wolf had found them. The brothers argued, Romulus killed Remus, and named the city after himself. This story tells us that Romans clearly admired children who were survivors. Romulus was said to have made a law that Romans should raise all their boys and the first-born girl.

The building of an extension to London's underground railroad meant cutting through a Roman layer of **archaeology.** It uncovered a road that had grooves in it made by the wheels of Roman carts, traces of a wood-lined tank for keeping oysters, a storage jar for fish sauce from Spain, and a pottery lamp shaped like a foot. Previous Roman remains found in London have included a woman's leather bikini.

Being Born

By law, Roman girls could marry at the age of twelve. The usual age was around fourteen. Girls were supposed to have children as soon as they married, and continue having more. It was believed that the younger the mother, the safer the birth would be. In fact giving birth was as risky for young girls as it was for older women whose bodies had been weakened by many births. More Roman women died in childbirth than Roman men were killed in war.

To live or to die?

Roman fathers wanted boys instead of girls. It was important to have a boy because he would inherit family property, carry on the family name, and care for the family's tombs. Because girls could not work, they could not add to the family income, and when they married, they had to be given a **dowry.** When a baby was born it was bathed and then placed at the father's feet. If the father picked it up, it meant he approved of it. The child was then accepted into the family.

Boy or girl, a baby had to be healthy and without defects or deformities. A family could legally abandon a baby and put it outside to die of hunger or cold. However, if someone decided to

This carving on a stone coffin in Rome shows a mother and a slave woman bathing a baby. It is possible that this coffin belongs to either a mother or a baby.

The *bulla*

A good luck charm called a *bulla* was hung around the neck of a newborn baby. The bulla protected the child against illness, accident and witchcraft. Romans believed that witches kidnapped and killed babies to use their body parts in making spells. In rich families the *bulla* was made of gold, in poor families it was leather. This would be worn until the child became an adult.

rescue an abandoned baby, they could not bring it up as a **slave** if it had been born free. However, **slave traders** often picked up abandoned babies anyway. Girls were more likely to be rejected, especially if a family already had a daughter. Sometimes children were sold to slave traders, or given to families needing to adopt an **heir,** simply because parents were too poor to raise them.

Dangerous years

The happy news of the birth of a healthy child was often painted on the outside wall of the family home. The whole neighborhood could then offer congratulations and prayers for good fortune. Out of every ten children born alive, approximately three would die before reaching their first birthday. Few would make it to the age of ten. This was because disease was common in busy Roman cities, and doctors knew less about curing diseases than they do today.

These *bullas* from the 4th century C.E. were worn by children born to rich parents.

Bringing Up Baby

Infant care

Our word "infant" comes from the Latin *"in fans"* meaning "without speech." Romans believed babies were like modeling clay that needed molding to the correct shape. So they were swaddled, or wrapped, tightly with cloths, especially around the joints. Their limbs were often put in splints to make them grow straight. The right hand was not bound in cloth to ensure that the child grew up right-handed. Left-handedness was thought to be unlucky.

Our word "sinister" means "evil," and is from the Latin for "left." Babies were also given daily cold baths to make them tough.

This tombstone was put up by a sad husband in memory of his wife, who died in childbirth. The **inscription** in Latin introduces her to the ghosts of the **Underworld**.

The high rate of infant death encouraged Roman mothers to make offerings to a whole range of **protective gods** and goddesses. These included Vaticanus, who opened a baby's mouth for its first scream, Vitumnus, who controlled breathing, Sentinus the senses, Ruminus breast-feeding, Potina drinking, and Educa eating. Cumina watched over cradles, and Parentia drove away things like bad dreams. Carna warded off stomach infections such as **dysentery,** which came from dirty water and was almost certainly a significant killer of babies. Romans blamed dysentery on evil spirits called *Strigae*. To keep them out, babies' bedrooms had narrow, slit windows guarded by sprigs of prickly hawthorn that the spirits would find hard to get past.

The *pedagogue*

Children in slave-owning households often had a male baby-sitter called a *pedagogue*. He would play with them, take them to the **public baths** and generally keep them out of trouble. He would teach them table manners and, if he could read, the alphabet. He would take the children to school and stay there, reporting back to their parents on their behavior. Romans believed in strict discipline. Even small children could expect to be punished for tantrums, sulking, or disobedience.

Nurses and nannies

Rich Roman women often refused to breast-feed their babies themselves. Instead, they hired wet nurses to do this for them. Soranus, a Greek doctor working in Rome, advised hiring a nurse who was at least twenty years old, with two or three children of her own. This would guarantee she was experienced and sensible. He also suggested Greek nurses, because it was thought that the baby would then grow up speaking Greek as well as Latin! A successful wet nurse might be kept on to become a nanny. A nanny is a woman who lives in a family's house and helps take care of the children. Divorce, the legal break-up of a marriage, was common among wealthy Romans, and children stayed with their father. This meant that many Roman children grew up closer to their nanny than to their mother.

Family Life

Our word "family" comes from the Latin *familia*, meaning household. A Roman household would include a married couple, their children, and often other relatives, such as older aunts, uncles, or cousins who did not have children of their own. A wealthy household would also have included **slaves** owned by the head of the family.

One big, happy family

Romans liked large families. Family members could help each other in work and **politics,** so the bigger a family, the richer and more powerful it could become. The more children one had, the better chance there was some would survive to look after their parents when they were old. Wealth, however, was no guarantee of health. Cornelia, mother of the

This Roman couple are shown with a young boy—possibly their adopted son.

LVIBIVSLFTRO VECILIAD LHILA

emperor Tiberius, had twelve babies, but only three survived to grow up.

When a grown child died as a teenager, poor parents felt that they had been cheated out of security in their old age. They also thought they had lost the time and money they had spent on bringing the child up for years. If a married couple failed to have children of their own, or lost them through illness or accident, they often adopted one or more.

Father knows best

In early Roman times, fathers had complete power over their families. They even had the right to kill their children if they were disobedient! Wherever possible, different generations lived together in the same house. The oldest living male was the head of the family. This meant that if a middle-aged man's father was still alive, he still had to get his father's permission for important decisions like getting married or selling a house or farm.

Mother dearest

The duty of the mother was to have children, bring them up, and organize the household. Respectable women did not leave the house much. They might go out to visit a female friend in her home, or take part in a religious ceremony for females. Slaves went out for the everyday shopping at the market and shops. Wives were expected to have as many children as possible. Every time a woman had a child, she risked dying. There were no clean hospitals to give birth in, and doctors and **midwives** did not have the knowledge that modern doctors have. Many wives died in their twenties or thirties, and so husbands might remarry two or three times. Divorce was allowed under Roman law, but when a couple separated, the children stayed with their father. This meant many children were brought up by stepmothers and, if the family was rich, by nurses or nannies.

House and Home

The rich

Wealthy children who lived in town were kept mostly at home for fear of disease, accident, or other harm. They lived in single-story houses with thick, high walls, and small, shuttered windows and a guarded doorway for security. Rooms ran round an open, airy courtyard (*atrium*) with a pool for rainwater. This would be a safe and shady place to play with toys, dolls, or pets such as dogs and cats. The dining room, used for entertaining, was usually the fanciest room in the house. There was often a study or library for the master of the house. Children were usually kept out of these rooms except on special occasions like family celebrations. Big houses had a rear courtyard (*peristyle*) with a garden, sometimes used as an outdoor dining room. The best houses had pipes that brought in water and underfloor central heating. Tile or **mosaic** floors were good for games like marbles.

Wealthy families usually had a country **villa** for summer. Here they could entertain friends, and get away from the heat and noise of the city. Children would have more freedom to play in the farmyard, go fishing, or hunt birds and small animals.

This villa in Pompeii would have belonged to a very wealthy family. Children would have plenty of room to play in the gardens here.

These items were found in a child's grave. Many Roman children died because of disease.

The poor

Most ordinary people who lived in town lived in apartment buildings. They were usually three or four floors in height, and known as *insulae* (islands). The ground floor, usually made of stone or brick, had stores, restaurants, and public toilets for residents. The higher floors were often not very sturdy. The poor families lived here, often in a single room. Space for children to play was very small. *Insulae* had no water supply, drainage, or heating. They were packed close together, and the air was poor. Sickness spread easily. Water came from public fountains, and waste was thrown out of the window into the street. Because of this, children risked catching illnesses in the dirty streets. Residents suffered from smoke, smells, noise, and danger from fire.

Meals

Most Romans lived in warm climates, and most food was eaten cold. Bread, fish, eggs, chicken, olives, fruit, nuts, and beans were basic foods. Only children and sick people drank milk, because most of it was used to make cheese. Older children drank wine or watered down vinegar. Butter was used to soothe babies with teething pains or mouth ulcers. At the main evening meal, wealthy adults ate while lying on couches. Children and the poor sat on stools. Even the rich ate with their fingers. Poor people ate take-out food from stores selling porridge, pies, fritters, soups, and sausages. This was because they had no kitchens at home.

Learning for Life

In the days of the Roman **republic,** fathers were supposed to take the time to educate their sons themselves, teaching them everything from writing to riding. Mothers and household **slaves** taught girls the domestic skills they needed to know at home.

After the Romans conquered Greece, they started to do things the way Greeks did. They began to send their sons to elementary school at the age of six or seven, until they were eleven or twelve. Girls might go too, but not past the age of twelve. Boys from wealthy families who expected them to go into **politics** continued studying for as many as ten more years. If they failed to do well, and were thought unfit to represent the family in the law courts or as a government official, they might be sent to live at a country **villa.** Here they would spend their lives overseeing the farm work.

The uses of literacy

It was thought that every free Roman male should be able to keep household accounts, read a **legal contract,** and keep written records of family prayers, remedies, and farming tips.

This Roman gravestone is from the 1st–2nd century C.E. Many people in ancient Rome were able to read the inscriptions on monuments such as this one.

Boys went to school to help them succeed in business and politics. The **Forum** in Pompeii was the town's business center.

Girls from wealthy families might also find reading and writing very helpful because that would show that their family was respectable. It was useful for girls to read and write because they could keep in touch with their friends and relatives by writing letters. They could also teach their daughters this useful skill. Because Latin was written without punctuation, it was necessary to read it aloud to make sure the reader understood where each sentence began and ended. Being able to read aloud meant being able to entertain, as well as help other members of the family.

Domestic skills

Girls had to learn how to cook, and how to make yarn from spinning thread and weave it into cloth. Girls in poorer families would actually need these skills when they got married. Girls of rich families would have a chef to cook for them, and could buy clothes for their family, rather than make them. But girls still had to know how these things were done. This would help them make sure their slaves were doing their work correctly. Even the daughters of the **emperor** himself were taught how to spin and weave.

Schools and Teachers

Primary

In elementary schools, children learned reading, writing, and arithmetic. The teacher was often an ex-slave, or disabled ex-soldier. Elementary school teachers were poorly paid, and not respected much by the general public. One Roman writer complained that by shouting at pupils arriving late, the teacher often woke up people nearby who were still trying to sleep! The teacher's pay depended on the number of pupils he could attract. Classes were usually small, with about twelve students to a class. In addition to fees, teachers also expected gifts at major **festivals.**

Romans believed that children would not like learning, and would therefore need to be beaten regularly. Paintings show a pupil lifted onto the back of one of his classmates to be beaten with a cane or eel-skin strap. Modern ideas about learning for fun, or through encouragement, would have seemed strange to Roman thinking.

Roman books, like the one held by the young man in the picture, were written on scrolls of **parchment** made from animal skins. Books were too expensive for children to have their own copies, so they would have to learn the text by heart.

What did writers say about school?

The Roman writer Quintilian said that children—particularly if they were the only child in the family—should be sent to school because if they stayed at home, they would grow up spoiled and rude. Another writer, Seneca, agreed—"A child will not stand up to hardships in life if he has not been denied anything and has always had his tears wiped away by his mother."

Schools were not in their own buildings. Lessons were given in the open air, or in a rented room, often at the back of a store. The teacher sat in a chair, the students on benches. The day lasted from dawn until early afternoon, with a break for lunch. Students did not have to go to school when there were religious festivals. They also had every ninth day off.

Learning at home

Boys from wealthy families active in **politics** had to learn both Latin and Greek. Many were taught by tutors at home. This did not necessarily mean learning alone. They were often part of a class consisting of brothers, cousins, the sons of neighbors, and even favored **slaves** who might go on to become secretaries, librarians, or family tutors themselves. Teachers at this level, dealing with boys aged from twelve until their late teens, were much better paid and treated with general respect.

Higher education

The third stage of education was public speaking, known as **rhetoric.** Very rich families might even send their sons to Athens or Crete to study under famous Greek teachers. The great Roman lawyer Cicero was a student until he was thirty. Public speaking was essential for those who wanted to enter public life as lawyers or politicians.

Lessons and Learning

Writing and reciting

The Roman alphabet was based on the Greek one, although the actual letters looked more like the ones used to write English today. The first thing children were taught was the Greek alphabet. This was because it was harder than Latin, and so then they would find learning the Latin alphabet easy. First they were taught the names of the letters. Then they would learn how to recite them from beginning to end. Then how to recite them backwards—and only then would they learn what the letters actually looked like!

At the bottom of this Roman coin are the letters SPQR which stand for Senate (Government) and People of Rome. The Latin is *Senatus Populusque Romanus*.

Writing equipment

Pupils learned writing on wooden boards that were covered with a thin layer of wax. Letters were scratched in with a pointed stick called a stylus. The flat end of the stylus was used for crossing out mistakes, and smoothing over the wax for re-use. More advanced students would learn to write on papyrus, a kind of paper imported from Egypt. They used a reed pen and ink made from soot and gum. Papyrus could be scrubbed clean and used several times.

Pupils were also expected to learn long sections of verse by heart, and recite them aloud. These were often stories about the gods or heroes from Roman history. They also learned rhymes about useful things, such as the value of different kinds of coin.

For children aged eleven and above, the curriculum concentrated on poetry and essay writing. There was also some geography, history, music, and **astronomy.** A lot of teaching consisted of the teacher asking a series of questions, and the pupil responding with correct answers they had to memorize.

Public speaking

Being able to speak clearly and forcefully was essential for those commanding soldiers, presenting cases in the law courts, and running for election to public office. Cicero, who became one of the greatest Roman public speakers, taught himself to overcome a stammer by practicing speaking with a stone in his mouth. This made him control his breathing and say each word clearly.

Students of **rhetoric** had to learn how to argue a point, train their memory, and use gestures and tricks of speech effectively. They memorized famous speeches and debated legal cases. One of the first public occasions on which a young man might try out his speaking skills would be making a speech in praise of a dead relative at their funeral.

Figure It Out

Children needed to know arithmetic to buy things in the market. Children of farmers, merchants, storekeepers, and craftsmen also needed to learn how to measure and weigh things as well. Children of rich families might also learn geometry because the Greeks did it, so it was fashionable. Boys wanting to follow in their father's footsteps as an architect, engineer, surveyor, or boat-builder also needed to learn geometry.

Mathematics

Romans used seven symbols to write numbers – I (=1) V (=5) X (=10) L (=50) C (=100) D (=500) and M (=1000). They could be used to write any other number, and were easier to carve in stone or wood than the numbers we use today. Roman numerals were written with the highest value on the left, and smallest on the right. Therefore MDCCCCLVIII = 1000 + 500 + (4 x 100) + 50 + 5 + (3 X 1) = 1958. When a smaller number symbol occurs to the left of a larger one it is subtracted: 9 is written IX, and 4 as IV. Numbers over one thousand were written by putting a line above a numeral. Multiplication and division were so difficult with Roman numerals, they were left to assistants. Merchants used a counting-board called an abacus, with vertical columns and counters to represent numbers.

This Roman merchant's abacus clearly shows the counters that represented numbers.

Weights and measures

The standard Roman unit of weight was the *libra* or pound. It was equivalent to about 12 ounces (327.45 grams). The Roman foot was equal to 11.65 modern inches (29.6 centimeters). Five feet were called one pace, and a thousand paces were one mile. The Roman mile equalled 1,618.5 yards (1,480 meters) and was therefore shorter than the modern mile of 1,760 yards (1,609 meters). Roman military roads were lined with milestones to help army commanders pace their soldiers' marching. It would have been important for children to understand weights and measures when they started work, or served across the **empire** in the Roman army.

This hoard of Roman coins is from the 1st–3rd century C.E..

Money

Another use for the arithmetic that Roman children learned would be in counting money. The smallest coin was an *as*. Four *as* coins made one *sestertius*, and four *sesterces* made one *denarius*. A small sack of wheat cost eight *sesterces*. A character in a novel by the writer Petronius described the importance of learning these things: "I didn't learn geometry and literary criticism and useless nonsense like that...I learned how to divide things into hundreds and work out percentages, and I know weights, measures, and currency."

Toys

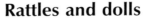

Rattles and dolls

Parents or other family members probably made most of their children's toys. Children in rich families might have toys made by skilled craftsmen. Babies were given clappers or rattles made of wood, clay pottery, or bone. Some had loose pebbles inside. Toddlers had wooden trolleys on wheels to push along to help them learn to walk.

Dolls were made out of cloth and wax. They often had movable arms and legs. Models and farmyard animals and pets were made out of clay, wood, or bronze. Metal hoops and wooden wheels were used for rolling along. Some hoops and wheels had bells on them so that they made a jingling noise. This also warned people to get out of the way!

Older children's toys

There were also play horses made from sticks with a head and reins and toy **chariots** with sails on to make them go faster. A rich child might have a chariot big enough to be pulled along by a goat or a pair of geese. At the other end of the scale were carts drawn by mice that were raced against each other. Marbles were made of pottery or glass. Country children often used hazelnuts or walnuts instead. Older children had whips and tops, kites, swings, see-saws, and go-carts. Boys fenced with wooden swords.

This Roman doll has movable joints, as do many dolls today. It is likely that this doll would have belonged to a child from a wealthy family.

Making a ball

Although rubber and plastics were unknown to the Romans, they did have ways to make balls that would bounce. One was to blow up a pig's bladder and wrap it tightly inside a protective outer cover of animal skin or leather. Another was to use catgut, or some other kind of animal muscle wound together like a ball of string, also covered with skin or leather. A third method was to use bits of natural sponge held together by string, and then wrapped in cloth. Sponge balls would not bounce as well as the other kinds, but were much easier to make.

Roman children played many different kinds of ball games, so balls were common. Some were hard, and used for bowling or catching. There were even balls made of glass. These were used in games that needed a high level of skill. Young children would probably not have been allowed to use them. Younger children played with soft balls made of rags, or hair wrapped inside linen, a type of material made from the flax plant.

This toy terrier dog came from a Roman site in Corbridge, England. It was offered to the gods as a sign of gratitude.

Games

Ball games

The names of many Roman ball games are known, but the exact rules are not. One children's game involved two concentric circles drawn on the ground. The inner circle was five feet across, and the outer one twenty feet across. Three or more players stood outside the outer ring and threw the ball to each other by bouncing it into the inner circle. If the ball was not caught one-handed, the thrower got a point. Whoever caught the ball threw it next. Players could run around the outer circle. The first player to score twenty-one points won the game.

The game *Trigon* involved three catchers standing in a triangle, twenty feet apart. It must have been a fast game because a separate player was needed for scoring. Sometimes two hard balls were in play at the same time. There may have been a rule about throwing with one hand and having to catch with the other. Points might also have been won for catching a ball and extra points won for palming it. Points were lost for dropping the ball, and the winning score was again twenty-one.

Evidence of many different kinds of games survives. Looking at this carving of children playing, from the 2nd century C.E., it is difficult to figure out the rules of the game.

Gambling, throwing and guessing

Children and adults played with dice. Gambling, or betting, was illegal, except during the **festival** of Saturnalia. Knucklebones was a favorite game with girls. These were long and narrow animal bones, with two flat faces, one concave, rounded inward, and one convex, rounded outward. The four faces were valued one, three, four, and six. Using four knucklebones, there were thirty-five scoring combinations a player could throw. The top score was when each bone thrown showed a different number—1, 3, 4, and 6.

Nuts were often used for throwing games. One involved trying to throw nuts into a narrow-necked container. Another required players to throw a nut onto a carefully arranged pile of nuts without making the pile collapse.

Another game involved two players each raising their right hand at the same time and guessing the total number of fingers raised by both players. There were also different kinds of board games. They either involved capturing pieces like modern chess, or racing counters to an end-point, like backgammon.

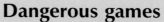

Dangerous games

The lawyer Cicero recorded a case in which boys playing in the street kicked a ball into a barber's shop. The man who was being shaved died after the startled barber cut his throat.

This **mosaic** shows men playing dice, possibly gambling. Children would also play dice, but would not gamble on their games.

Sports

Taking part

The Romans had immense respect for Greek learning, but unlike the Greeks, they did not make competitive sport a major part of education. Boys, however, were expected to take part in sports in their free time. These included such Greek favorites as wrestling, boxing, and throwing the javelin. They also played very rough games. One involved two boys holding either end of a long rope, then running after two others, trying to tie them up. The other two had sticks to beat off the boys trying to rope them in. In the countryside, hunting was used to build up toughness, test bravery against wild animals, and gain skill with a spear. Horseback riding was done without stirrups, the rings that hold the rider's feet in place.

The boy at the bottom of this carving (right) is shown watching the chariot races.

28

Spectators

As the **empire** grew richer, the Romans began to leave serious sport to professionals. Fights between **gladiators** began as a form of human **sacrifice** at the funeral of an important person. Under the empire, gladiatorial games were big business. They were usually held at religious **festivals.** Many gladiators were criminals or **prisoners of war,** the rest were **slaves.** A tough teenage boy slave might be picked out by his owner to train as a future gladiator. Although becoming a gladiator was very dangerous, it did offer a small hope of fame, freedom, and fortune.

Boy racers

Chariot racing was as popular as watching gladiators, and almost as dangerous. Races between four different teams—the Reds, Blues, Whites, and Greens—might involve up to twelve chariots. Crashes were frequent and often deadly. Whichever chariot finished first won—even without its driver! Top charioteers were like super-heroes. Many of the drivers were just boys when they began. Some started as young as twelve. Young charioteers were valued because the lighter the charioteer, the faster the chariot could travel. In a ten-year career ending with his death at the age of twenty-two, African-born charioteer Crescens took part in 680 races. He won 47 victories, and prize money of 1,558,346 *sesteraces*.

The Colosseum in Rome could hold 50,000 spectators. Boys were taken to gladiator fights here to toughen them up.

The World of Work

Helping at home

Regular jobs for children included looking after younger brothers and sisters, keeping the fire going, fetching water, and grinding grain to make flour. In the countryside they also gathered firewood, nuts, berries, and mushrooms, cleared stones from fields, and helped to harvest grapes and olives.

Following mom and dad

Most boys were brought up to do the same job as their father did, learning the trade from him. There were few jobs outside the home for women—storekeeper, bath attendant, needlewoman, shepherdess, or midwife, a woman who helps other women have babies. Most girls learned housekeeping skills from their mother. **Inscriptions** found on tombs show that some girls worked from a very young age: "In memory of Pieris, a hairdresser. She lived nine

The children in this banqueting scene from Pompeii are slaves. They are shown serving the adults.

years. Her mother put up this headstone."

Slavery

Slavery was common throughout the Roman world. A child born to a **slave** mother was by law a slave, even if the father was free. Some slaves were captured **prisoners of war.** Others, often children, were bought from **slave traders** who had kidnapped them.

Household slaves

Most Roman households would have included slaves. These may also have included children who would have helped with cleaning and worked in the kitchen. In some houses, they would have been taught to read and write so they could be used for skilled jobs in later life. Many slaves were treated as valued members of the family and given positions of trust such as physician (doctor), teacher, bookkeeper, or bodyguard. Others were musicians, hairdressers, and cooks.

Industrial slaves

Slaves were often used for dirty, dangerous, or exhausting work such as farming, making bricks, building, and mining. Slave children were especially useful in mining for crawling through narrow tunnels. Mine slaves were cruelly treated, and had many accidents. Runaway slaves who were caught could be branded, or marked with a piece of hot iron, or executed. Slaves were often forced to wear an iron collar around their neck to show that they were slaves.

Clothes and Fashions

Roman clothing changed very little over a thousand years. Most children wore simple clothes of wool and linen, made at home by their mothers or **slaves.** The rich bought cloth that was already made, and could afford dyed materials and cottons from India. Cotton and silk were much lighter and more comfortable in warm climates, and could be washed and dried more easily. Women wore lighter, brighter colors and more patterns than men did. Children dressed even more simply than adults did, in loose **tunics,** sandals, and cloaks. Girls usually only wore white until they were married. In cold climates, like Roman Britain, furs and felt, a cloth made from cotton or wool, were worn.

This **mosaic**, from Carthage, shows a young boy dressed in a short tunic.

The toga

When a boy wore a **toga** for the first time, it meant he was an adult. The toga was a large half-circle of thick white wool which had to be draped and folded with great care. Only adult male Roman **citizens** were allowed to wear a toga. A slave usually helped his master put it on, but it was awkward and heavy to wear. Most men preferred a tunic for everyday use. Some emperors passed laws ordering men to wear a toga on formal occasions.

Garments

Because needles made of bronze or bone were rather clumsy, Roman clothes usually required little sewing. Boys and girls both wore **loincloths** as underwear, and a short tunic gathered at the waist. In warm weather, tunics served as pajamas as well. In colder weather, they were used as underwear, and another heavier tunic was worn on top. In winter and wet weather, cloaks, often with hoods, were worn.

There were no buttons, and garments were held together with belts, drawstrings, or pins. Children might carry knucklebones in the folds of their clothes. Coins were small and often carried in the mouth because garments had no pockets.

Fashion

Women wore robes reaching down to their ankles. They often covered their head with a veil, scarf, or shawl outdoors to protect their hairstyle. Some wore wigs. These were made from black human hair brought over from India, or cut off from one of their own blond **slaves.** Rich ladies with lots of free time spent hours on their appearance. Girls would learn from their mother or her maid how to choose jewelry, arrange their hair, and put on makeup and perfume.

Keeping Clean and Healthy

Hygiene at home

In Roman **mythology,** Hygieia, goddess of health, was the daughter of Aesculapius, god of healing. Her name gives us the word "hygiene." Although larger houses had pools and fountains for washing, most children would not have had a bathroom in their own homes. Toilets would often have been shared between families, particularly in poorer areas. People would have visited the **public baths,** where they could keep clean, meet friends, and play ball or board games.

The public baths

Wherever possible, the Romans built public bath houses. These were used by the whole family. Children were allowed in free. The grandest baths had lead-lined pools, marble walls, **mosaic** floors, statues, and fountains. Bath houses were leisure, fitness, and social centers with their own exercise yard, gymnasium, covered walks, gardens, and stores. Children could keep fit at the same time as they kept clean. Cakes, biscuits, sausages, and drinks were sold from street stalls.

The *palaestrum* (gym) at Pompeii is where young men prepared for athletic events. They used the large swimming pool on the right.

Even children of rich families, with baths at home, went to the public baths. Most people went daily, women usually in the morning, and men in the afternoon after work. Children would probably have gone during the day, unless they were working. Daily bathing probably helped prevent skin diseases and heal minor cuts.

Before washing themselves in the baths, children would do some exercise in the gymnasium attached to the baths. They might practice wrestling, or throwing a ball to one another. The Romans believed that regular exercise was an important part of staying healthy.

Health and death
Children, especially in dirty, overcrowded slums, could die from infectious diseases that were especially common in hot weather. In poor country areas, bad harvests caused deaths from starvation. Other dangers that could be deadly included snakebites and accidents causing major wounds or broken bones. Most families were too poor to afford a doctor or lived too far away from one. Children relied on their parents to treat them with medicines made from herbs, oil, vinegar, and honey.

Beliefs and Behavior

Inside the family home

The whole family would have been expected to worship the household gods every day. Each household had its own **shrine** for family worship, led by the father. The shrine was called the *lararium*. Boys would learn what to do by copying their father, and when they grew up, they would have to lead their own family's worship. Girls might join their mother in making an offering to Vesta, goddess of the **hearth,** who was especially important to housewives.

A Genius stands in the center of this shrine to the household gods, wearing a veil for offering a sacrifice.

Respect was shown to the gods by sacrificing animals or birds. If a bird or animal was sacrificed, it means it was killed to honor the gods. They would also make offerings of **incense,** bread, fruit, or wine, and say prayers. Families were also watched over by a guardian spirit, and the spirits of their **ancestors.** Portraits or wax **death masks** of ancestors were placed around the *atrium*. Children's first experiences of religion would come from these ceremonies inside the home.

Children and the gods

The gods of the official religion were honored at temples, and by public ceremonies in which children also took part. These usually involved a procession, then a **sacrifice** and prayers. Children learned the **myths** about the gods' adventures and quarrels. Many of the Roman gods they learned about were the same as those of ancient Greece but they had different names. Zeus, the Greek king of the gods, was renamed Jupiter by the Romans. Hera, his wife, became Juno.

Romans were great believers in omens, or signs. They believed that natural signs, like the sudden appearance of an eagle, were a warning of important events, such as an earthquake or the death of the **emperor.** They also believed in telling the future by examining the entrails (intestines and bowels) of sacrificed birds.

Holidays and Festivals

Family occasions

Families could have their own private **festivals** including birthdays, the day the son of the house spoke his first word, or the return of a household member from a journey. Travel was correctly seen as risky, particularly when it involved a voyage by sea.

Public holidays

Religious festivals were usually public holidays, although business was only forbidden on the most solemn occasions. Festivals usually included games, races, and performances of plays. Some of the most important festivals for children and families were:

January 1st—bulls were sacrificed to Jupiter for his protection

February 13th–21st—past family members' tombs were honored with flowers, food, and wine

March 15th—families celebrated the goddess of the year with picnics

April 21st—bonfires and street parties honored the day Rome was founded

June 24th—boating parties and picnics honored Fortuna, goddess of luck

August 13th—**slaves** got a day off in honor of Diana, goddess of hunting.

This child holding a goat for **sacrifice** is shown wearing a *bulla* around his neck.

Winter festival

The middle of winter was a time of special celebration for parents and their children. The festival of *Saturnalia* extended over a number of days starting on December 17th. It was a time for families to get together and presents were exchanged. Slaves were given special privileges and, for one day, changed places with their masters.

This wall painting from Ostia, Italy, shows children taking part in a religious festival.

In addition to regular festivals, there might be other ones to celebrate a victory in war, or to ask the aid or mercy of the gods in a disaster. Villages celebrated fertility gods and goddesses to mark plowing, sowing, harvesting, and other important times of the agricultural calendar. Farmers led animals around their field boundaries in a procession, then sacrificed them while praying to the gods to ward off diseases, storms, or drought. Children would have celebrated the harvest as well as adults—it was important for everyone that there was plenty of food to eat.

Lupercalia

Many festivals continued even after Rome became Christian. At *Lupercalia* (February 15th) sacrifices were made at the Lupercal, the cave where the wolf sheltered Romulus and Remus. Then young men in goat skin costumes ran through Rome, admired by young girls. In 494 C.E. Pope Gelasius I banned Christians from taking part in this festival because he did not approve of it. Instead, he made the day a festival in honor of the Virgin Mary.

All Grown Up

Coming of age

A free Roman boy passed to manhood between the age of fourteen and seventeen. The special ceremony of putting on a man's **toga** usually took place in the **forum** at the **festival** of *Liberalia* on March 17th. Before going there he would offer his *bulla*, and the **tunic** he wore as a boy to the gods at the household altar. The whiskers from the new adult's first shave were put in a thin, glass jar called a phial and left at the **temple** of Apollo as an offering. Then he went to a government office to register as a **citizen,** which made him responsible for military service and allowed him to vote. Then came a party at home to celebrate. A young man could not hold important public positions until he was thirty and had done ten years of military service.

Getting married

Girls became women when they became wives. The night before her wedding, the bride offered her favorite dolls and toys to the gods at her household **shrine.** Interestingly, Roman dolls were usually made to look like brides, not babies.

A bronze statue of a Roman soldier from the 2nd century C.E. is now in the British Museum. He is wearing an iron helmet, a leather skirt, and heavy sandals.

In this engraving of a Roman wedding ceremony, from the 2nd century C.E., the groom holds the bride's hand.

Parents, especially among wealthy or politically powerful families, usually arranged marriages. Husbands were usually grown men, while brides were normally in their early teens. Engagements were marked with a party and a marriage contract. The contract set out the terms of the **dowry** of cash or land given with the bride. The bride was given a ring that she wore on the third finger of the left hand. This was because Romans believed that there was a nerve there leading straight to the heart.

The wedding day had to be chosen to avoid unlucky dates. April and the second half of June were considered especially favorable. On the big day the bride braided her hair and put on a headdress of flowers, a white tunic, and a flame-red veil. Her family home was decorated with flowers and ribbons. When the groom arrived, a priest performed a ritual to make sure the day was still lucky. After an exchange of vows and the signing of the wedding contract, the chief bridesmaid joined the hands of the newlyweds. They then prayed to the gods for their blessing. After a party at the bride's home, everybody went in procession to the groom's home, accompanied by torch-bearers and musicians. When they arrived, the groom carried the bride over the threshold and their new life together began.

How Do We Know?

◀▷ ◀▷ ◀▷ ◀▷ ◀▷ ◀▷ ◀▷ ◀▷ ◀▷ ◀▷ ◀▷ ◀▷ ◀▷ ◀▷

The problem of the past

Historians try to recapture the past out of what people wrote, made, built, or buried. Most of what the Romans wrote or made is lost forever. Common items of wood or wax, clay or cloth, horn, bone, or leather are most likely to have rotted. The same is true of papyrus, paper made from plants, or **parchment,** a writing surface made from animal skin. Much of what has survived has come from late in Roman history, and from Roman Egypt and North Africa, where the dry climate has preserved many objects and manuscripts.

Tombs and treasures

One direct form of evidence about Roman childhood is the burials, bodies, and belongings of children themselves. Babies less than forty days old were often just buried under the floor of the house. In the countryside, where most people lived, child burials were also simple. Little evidence survives about these kinds of children. Rich children, however, were buried in fine stone tombs that often preserved their remains far better. The tombs often contained

This miniature glass bowl was part of the grave goods belonging to a young girl buried in the 3rd century C.E.. It is amazing that the bowl remains in such good condition.

favorite dolls, toys, and, in the case of infants, feeding bottles.

On display in the Museum of London are the grave goods found with a young girl who was buried early in the 3rd century C.E. Her parents had buried with her a pair of earrings made of loops of twisted gold wire, and a bronze coin that had been worn as a pendant on a necklace. She also had two white clay figures of the goddess of Venus, an ivory statuette, a miniature glass bowl, and a tiny carved bone jar with a lid.

Some tombs have carved portraits. One shows a little girl holding her favorite pet cat. Sometimes pets were buried with the child. We know much more about rich, powerful, educated Romans—because they had more and could do more—than we do about the poor who outnumbered them by millions. The most common type of Roman ever to have lived was a child who died before they could have children of their own.

A father's grief

Inscriptions on tombs show how sad parents were when children had died as teenagers, having survived childhood illnesses. In a letter to a friend, the writer Pliny described how, after the invitations had been sent out, a thirteen year old girl's father was: "spending on incense, perfumes and spices for her funeral what he had planned to spend on gowns, pearls, and jewels for her wedding." Her family must have been wealthy for her father to plan such a wedding.

A pair of earrings with twisted gold wire were found also in the grave dating from the 3rd century C.E. The grave was found in London.

Timeline

753   The city of Rome is founded.

c.600   Latin becomes a written language.

509   The last Roman king is overthrown in favor of a republic.

312   Building work begins on the Via Appia, Rome's first great road.

241–225 Rome conquers Sicily, Sardinia, and Corsica.

206   Rome conquers Iberia (Spain).

149–146 Rome defeats Carthage and conquers North Africa.

146   Greece becomes part of the Roman empire.

91–88   Civil wars lead to Roman citizenship for all Italians.

58–50   Julius Caesar conquers Gaul.

44   Julius Caesar is murdered.

29   Egypt becomes part of the Roman empire.

27   Augustus becomes the first Roman emperor.

C.E.

14   Augustus dies.

64   Rome is devastated by fire.

73   A major slave uprising is led by Spartacus.

79   The eruption of Vesuvius buries the cities Pompeii and Herculaneum.

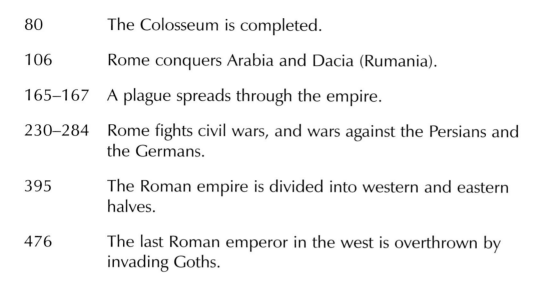

More Books to Read

Chapman, Gillian. *The Romans*. Chicago: Heinemann Library, 1998.

Corbishley, Mike. *Growing Up in Ancient Rome*. Mahwah, N.J.: Troll Communications, LLC, 1997.

Dixon, Suzanne. *Childhood, Class, and Kin in the Roman World*. New York: Routledge, 2001.

Ganeri, Anita. *The Ancient Romans*. Austin, Tex.: Raintree Steck-Vaughn Publishers, 2000.

MacDonald, Fiona. *I Wonder Why Romans Wore Togas: And Other Questions about Ancient Rome*. New York: Houghton Mifflin Company, 1997.

Shuter, Jane. *The Ancient Romans*. Chicago: Heinemann Library, 1998.

Wroble, Lisa A. *Kids in Ancient Rome*. New York: The Rosen Publishing Group, Inc., 1999.

Glossary

ancestor family member from long ago

archaeology study of objects and evidence from the past

astronomy study of the stars and planets

barbarian person who did not respect Roman ways

chariot two-wheeled cart used for racing or warfare

citizen Roman man entitled to vote in elections and serve in the army

death mask portrait made from a wax mold of a dead person's face

dowry gift to the person getting married from the family

emperor supreme ruler of Rome

empire large area with many peoples living under rule of an emperor

excavation digging to uncover items from the past

festival celebration, usually in honor of a god

forum large open square in a Roman city, used for public meetings

Germanic something from Germany

gladiator trained professional fighter who fought in the Roman arena

hearth place for a fire

heir person who inherits money and land

hobbyhorse toy made of a long stick with reins and a horse's head

incense something burned to produce a sweet smell

inscription writing cut into wood or stone, usually on a gravestone

legal contract agreement that can be enforced by a law court

loincloth simple form of underwear, a strip of cloth wound around the waist

mosaic decorative picture made up of tiny pieces of colored tile

mythology and **myths** ancient stories about gods or heroes

parchment a surface for writing on, made from animal skin

politics taking part in the decisions made by government

prisoner of war person captured in battle

protective god god who prevents harm

public bath baths open to everyone

republic form of government in early Rome, with elected officials, not a king

rhetoric art of speaking well in public

sacrifice living thing killed in honor of a god

shrine place where gods are worshiped

slave servant who was not free, and who belonged to a master

slave trader person who bought and sold slaves

stylus pointed stick used for writing on wax

temple building used for religious purposes

toga Roman garment, like a loosely folded cloak

tunic sleeveless knee-length garment, often pulled in at the waist

Underworld dark and gloomy place to which Romans believed people went after death

villa large country house

Index